FIRENADOES
Tornadoes of fire

Written by Mike

T0364582

Contents

Collins

1 Firenado! The deadliest fire

Have you ever seen a tornado in real life, on television or in films? If you have, then you'll know they are deadly, funnel-shaped clouds that appear during violent storms. They whirl around **ferociously** and can suck up people, buildings, cars and trees.

Now, imagine a fire that gets out of control – a wildfire. Strong winds blow and suddenly the flames rise up. They begin to look like a tornado. This is a terrifying fire whirl – or, as it's sometimes known, a **firenado**!

Like a tornado, it can also suck up people and things. But firenadoes suck them into flames. Brutal blazes like firenadoes are on the increase. But why? And how do they begin?

The world has always had wildfires. But what exactly *is* a wildfire? Usually, it means a fire that is uncontrolled, unplanned and unwanted! Such a blaze is sometimes called a "bushfire" or "forest fire", as most fires begin in these places.

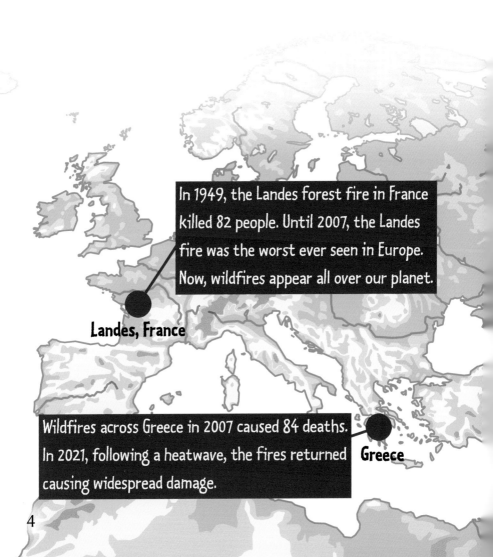

In 1949, the Landes forest fire in France killed 82 people. Until 2007, the Landes fire was the worst ever seen in Europe. Now, wildfires appear all over our planet.

Landes, France

Wildfires across Greece in 2007 caused 84 deaths. In 2021, following a heatwave, the fires returned causing widespread damage.

Greece

There were even wildfires about 400 million years ago before humans appeared. These fires would have been caused by lightning or volcanoes.

Over the last 150 years, there have been many serious wildfires.

Wildfires aren't new — but they are getting worse.

The powerful Mari wildfires in Russia in 1921 destroyed pine forest and 60 villages. In August 2021 similar fires returned, forcing hundreds of people to leave their homes.

Mari, Russia

2 What is the fire triangle?

Firefighters say there are three things that create wildfires. These are **fuel**, **oxygen** and a heat **source**. They call it the "fire triangle".

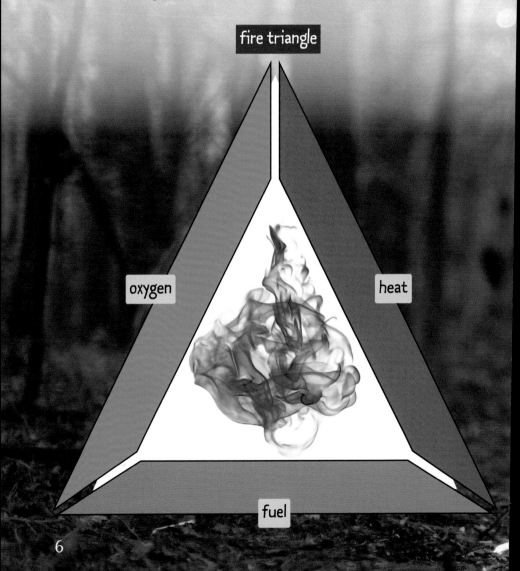

fire triangle

oxygen

heat

fuel

In simple terms, imagine you wanted to light a fire on a camping trip. You'd probably gather dry wood (this would be your fuel). Then, you'd strike a match (your heat source). Air has oxygen in it so your fire would probably start without your help. However, when you blow on fire, it increases the flow of oxygen. This would probably make the fire burn more brightly.

Wildfires are just extreme versions of a campfire.

3 What causes a wildfire?

Sadly, most fires start because of human actions. These can be accidental – for example, someone dropping a lit cigarette, or forgetting to put out a barbecue. Or they could be caused by a spark from a machine. However, sometimes people start wildfires deliberately. This is a crime called **arson** and punishments can be very severe.

Fires begin naturally, too. During a storm, lightning sometimes strikes trees and sets them on fire. Lightning is a hot, electrical current which shoots out of storm clouds. Electricity searches for the easiest route to the ground. Trees are more likely to be struck because they are tall. They are then good conductors and offer little resistance because they contain a lot of water.

You can sometimes spot trees that have been struck by lightning because they have a black scar down their sides or have been split in two.

8

9

4 Why are there so many wildfires in forests?

Fires often start beneath or on the surface of the forest floor. Ground fires burn buried vegetation such as **peat**. Surface fires tend to burn dried leaves, twigs and low-level plants. These surface fires carry more risk as they can lead to intense fires.

When strong winds combine with fire and flames, the surface fire climbs the tree as if it were a ladder. Eventually, it reaches the top (the "crown") of the tree or the tops of many trees (the "canopy"). Burning spreads very rapidly.

This is called a crown fire which is very destructive.

canopy

crown

ladder effect

5 A town called Paradise

Wildfires in California, USA, aren't new. However, in 2018, a small town called Paradise hit the news when it was totally destroyed by a wildfire, killing 86 people.

How did this tragedy occur?

Firstly, years of **drought** meant that everywhere was dry and there were lots of dead trees.

Secondly, there was a wind of 113 kilometres per hour. It was also coming from a northerly direction and Paradise was right in its path.

Finally, Paradise's position at the top of a ridge with valleys all around meant there was only one escape road out of town.

So, when a spark from a nearby power line started the fire, Paradise was in terrible danger.

Some people even saw a firenado – a towering whirlwind of fire.

6 Kangaroo Island and the Australian fires

Wildfires have also affected many other parts of the world, such as Australia.

In 2020, Kangaroo Island was hit by a devastating fire. The island has a world-famous animal **reserve** where you can see koalas, kangaroos and the rare glossy black **cockatoo**.

At one point, flames were 48 kilometres wide, and over 90 metres high and moved at 97 kilometres per hour. Roughly half of the island was destroyed.

However, nature is capable of fighting back, as the picture on the right shows. These yacca trees on Kangaroo Island, which have been blackened by fire damage, are already growing back.

And people came together to raise money to help those who live on the island. A wildlife rescue centre has helped save wounded koalas.

The whole community fought back against this deadly danger.

7 Fighting fires

In many countries, **volunteer** firefighters protect their local area. This means they aren't full-time firefighters and some don't get paid. Yet they face many dangers.

In the state of New South Wales in Australia, nearly 90 per cent of the firefighters are volunteers.

Years ago, they would be called out mostly for small fires. Now, they have to deal with larger blazes like the ones on Kangaroo Island. They use **tankers** and might have to pump out as much as 1,800 litres of water per minute. That's a *lot* of water.

As well as traditional tankers, there are some more modern inventions that help fight fires.

tanker

Wildland fire engines

What are they?

They are a cross between a truck and a fire engine with
four-wheel drive suitable for rough **terrain**. There are many
different types which vary in size and equipment.

How do they help?

Because they are smaller than normal fire engines or tankers,
they can get to remote places. They can also spray water while
they are on the move.

wildland fire engine

Drones

What are they?

Drones are flying machines without pilots
that are controlled remotely from
a safe place. Those used to help
with fires shoot out flames
or little balls of
chemicals which
start instant fires.

drone

How do they help?

They are used to quickly
burn off shrubs and plants
in remote areas. This way
there is less "fuel" on the ground.
As you'll remember, surface fires
can quickly lead to bigger fires.
Controlled burning of surface
fuel means there is less for
bigger fires to burn.

balls filled with chemicals

Airtankers

What are they?

Also called "water bombers", they are aeroplanes with huge water tanks. They can be filled on the ground, or some **amphibious** craft can scoop up water from lakes or reservoirs.

airtanker

How do they help?

They fly above burning forests and drop large amounts of water.

8 Fire-chasers!

As well as firefighters, there are also people who choose
to "chase" fires. They are similar to "storm-chasers".
These are people who drive cars or trucks around in search
of storms. Sometimes they want to take amazing photographs.
Others want to help by gathering information about weather in
order to warn people if a storm is on its way. Either way, it's
a very dangerous activity.

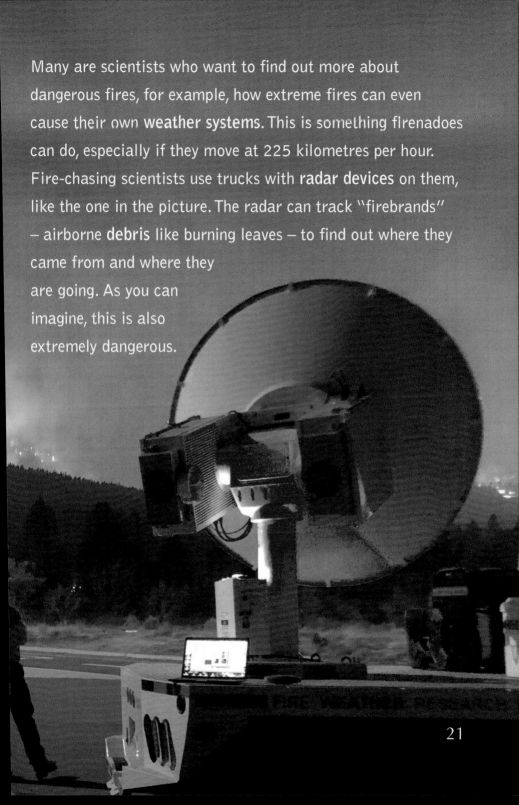

Many are scientists who want to find out more about dangerous fires, for example, how extreme fires can even cause their own **weather systems**. This is something firenadoes can do, especially if they move at 225 kilometres per hour. Fire-chasing scientists use trucks with **radar devices** on them, like the one in the picture. The radar can track "firebrands" – airborne **debris** like burning leaves – to find out where they came from and where they are going. As you can imagine, this is also extremely dangerous.

9 Why are wildfires on the increase?

Scientists, like the fire-chasers, are worried about the increase in wildfires. Why have such fires increased?

One reason is climate change. Earth's temperature has risen by about 1.5 degrees Celsius in the last 250 years. This may not sound a lot, but this slight rise has been linked to an increase in extreme weather events, such as **hurricanes** and other powerful storms (for example, those with tornadoes in them). So, there are more strong winds and the ground is hotter.

Another reason is that human beings now live in lots of places which were once wild, so fires are now very close by.

Another issue is logging – cutting down trees to make space for farming, or to turn into paper and other products. The grass that replaces the trees is drier and more likely to catch alight.

22

10 How do scientists find out about wildfires?

One way is simple: people see serious fires for themselves and tell others about them. For example, storm-chasers and fire-chasers see wildfires and report their location.

Then, there are media organisations (newspapers and television stations) who also report them.

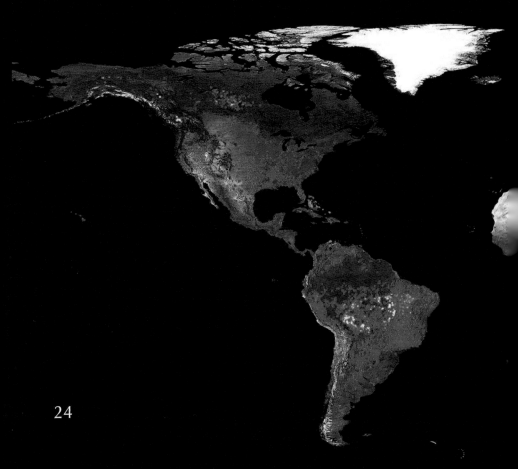

Weather organisations like the **Meteorological Office** observe them through the use of **satellites** and weather stations.

And NASA (the American space agency) even keeps a track of them across the world. Using images taken from Terra, NASA's satellite, fire maps like the one below show actively burning fires around the world and are updated monthly.

Look at the image below from September 2020. Can you see where most fires were at this time?

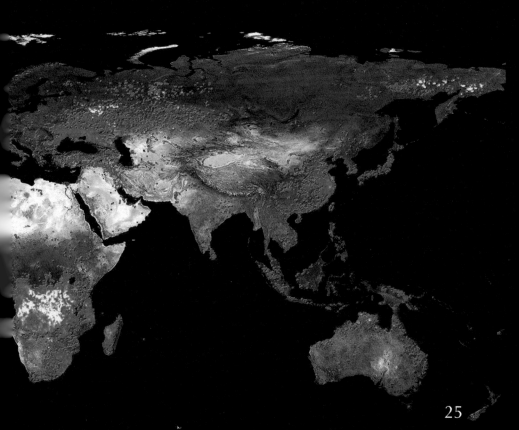

11 Why is it important to know about wildfires?

Wildfires are a **symptom** of global warming. And if we want to reduce global warming, which is damaging the planet, then we need to reduce wildfires, among other things.

And we can all do our bit to stop fires beginning in the place where it really matters: the countryside.

Top tips

Avoid having open fires in woodland, especially when it's dry, windy and hot.

If you have a barbecue, make sure it's in a safe and suitable area. Don't leave it unattended.

Take empty bottles and glass home with you. Sun can shine through glass and **ignite** dry grass or wood.

Keep pets away from any open fires.

If you see a fire

Don't try to tackle it yourself, but report it immediately to Fire and Rescue services or a responsible adult.

Leave the area as quickly as possible, in a downhill direction if you can, as fire usually travels upwards.

Glossary

amphibious suited to both land and water

arson setting fire to something on purpose

cockatoo a type of parrot

debris scattered pieces of rubbish

drought period of very dry weather

ferociously violently

firenado fire which has been whipped up into a funnel like a tornado

fuel material which produces heat or power

hurricanes storms with a violent wind

ignite cause to catch fire

Meteorological Office organisation that monitors the weather and climate

NASA short for National Aeronautics and Space Administration

oxygen a gas which is essential to life

peat vegetation which has decomposed into a brown, earthy mass

radar devices machines or systems that can identify signs of heat

reserve a protected area for animals

satellites equipment orbiting Earth to monitor weather

source the place something begins

symptom sign of something wrong

tankers lorries which carry fuel or water

terrain land

volunteer someone who offers unpaid help

weather systems movements of warm or cold air across Earth

Index

What causes wildfires?

cigarettes

unattended barbecues or fires

strong winds or storms

rise in global temperatures

logging

lightning strikes

electrical sparks

building development

 Ideas for reading

Written by Gill Matthews
Primary Literacy Consultant

Reading objectives:
- ask questions to improve their understanding of a text
- identify main ideas drawn from more than one paragraph and summarise these
- retrieve and record information from non-fiction

Spoken language objectives:
- ask relevant questions to extend their understanding and knowledge
- use relevant strategies to build their vocabulary
- maintain attention and participate actively in collaborative conversations, staying on topic and initiating and responding to comments

Curriculum links: Art; Geography – Locational knowledge

Interest words: damaging, reduce, avoid, suitable, unattended

Resources: IT, atlas

Build a context for reading

- Ask children to look at the front cover of the book. Discuss what they can see and ask what they think *firenadoes* are. Read the back-cover blurb. Ask what kind of book this is and what the children think they will find out from the book.

- Discuss the kinds of features that are often found in non-fiction books, for example, contents, glossary, index. Explore children's knowledge and understanding of these features. Give them time to skim the book to find out which features are included in this book.

Understand and apply reading strategies

- Read pp2–5 aloud. Ask children to summarise what they have learnt from this chapter about firenadoes and wildfires. If necessary, model how to summarise by identifying the main points of each chapter.

- Give children time to look up words in bold in the glossary.